HAMPSHIRE RAILWAYS

IN OLD PHOTOGRAPHS

HAMPSHIRE RAILWAYS

IN OLD PHOTOGRAPHS

COLLECTED BY

KEVIN ROBERTSON

ALAN SUTTON

Alan Sutton Publishing Limited
Phoenix Mill · Thrupp · Stroud · Gloucestershire

First published 1989
Reprinted 1997
Copyright © Kevin Robertson 1989

British Library Cataloguing in Publication Data

Hampshire railways in old photographs.
1. Hampshire. Railway services, history
I. Robertson, Kevin
385'.09422'7

ISBN 0-86299-668-6

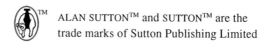

ALAN SUTTON™ and SUTTON™ are the
trade marks of Sutton Publishing Limited

Typesetting and origination by
Alan Sutton Publishing
Printed in Great Britain by
WBC, Bridgend, Mid Glam.

INTRODUCTION

Compared with the industrial Midlands and north, Hampshire is very much a rural community with rolling downs and heathland, perhaps the best known of which is the picturesque New Forest. Into this environment 150 years ago came the railway builders and, slowly at first, they began to weave their steel rails across this previously unspoilt landscape to form the transport system that still survives today.

In this compilation of views of Hampshire railways I have been fortunate in being able to use a number that I have collected over the years as a result of other projects and so these will see the light of day for the first time. Following on from the earlier volume on *Wiltshire Railways in Old Photographs*, I have adopted the same format and intermingled various paperwork items as I do think it is important to take a wider look at the whole question of railway history.

Unfortunately some stations and locations are still photographically obscure; Hurn and Barton Stacey Halt are just two examples. I have also made a deliberate, although personally painful, decision to avoid any coverage of the former DN & S line in the present volume. This has had more than its fair share of paper in recent years and as a result more space can be devoted to other areas.

I must express my gratitude to Reg, Derek and Dennis for their help and also Dennis Tillman for producing the map.

Kevin Robertson

The following books and magazines have been consulted:

The Railways of Gosport, Kevin Robertson.
The Southsea Railway, Kevin Robertson.
A Regional History of the Railways of Southern England, H.P. White.
The London & South Western Railway, R.A. Williams.
A Gazetteer of the Railway Contractors, Lawrence Popplewell.
The Southern Railway Magazine.

Opening of lines in date order.

11.5.1840	London to Southampton
28.11.1841	Bishopstoke to Gosport
1.3.1847	Bishopstoke to Salisbury
14.6.1847	Chichester to Portsmouth
1.6.1847	Southampton to Dorchester
1.9.1848	Fareham to Cosham
1.11.1848	Reading to Basingstoke
4.7.1849	Reading to Farnborough
28.7.1852	Farnham to Alton
3.7.1854	Basingstoke to Andover
1.5.1857	Andover to Salisbury
12.7.1858	Brockenhurst to Lymington
1.1.1859	Portsmouth Railway (To Havant)
13.11.1862	Ringwood to Christchurch
6.4.1863	Stokes Bay Branch
1.6.1863	Botley to Bishop's Waltham
1.9.1864	Petersfield to Midhurst
6.3.1865	Andover to Redbridge
2.10.1865	Alton to Winchester
5.3.1866	Southampton to Netley
16.7.1867	Havant to Hayling Island
14.3.1870	Christchurch to Bournemouth
26.9.1871	Southampton Royal Pier Extension
15.6.1874	Poole to Bournemouth
2.10.1876	Portsmouth Waterside Extension
5.2.1883	Swindon to Andover
1.5.1884	Lymington Harbour Extension
1.5.1885	Newbury to Winchester
1.6.1885	Hurstbourne to Fullerton
1.7.1885	Fratton to East Southsea
5.3.1888	Brockenhurst to Christchurch
2.9.1889	Netley to Fareham
1.10.1891	Winchester (DNS) to Shawford Junction
12.5.1894	Fort Brockhurst to Lee-on-the-Solent
1.6.1901	Basingstoke to Alton
1.6.1903	Alton to Fareham
11.12.1905	Bentley to Borden
10.1906	Longmoor Military Railway
20.7.1925	Totton to Fawley

FARNBOROUGH STATION on the main London to Southampton railway. This was one of the early stations on the main line, although it is shown here after quadrupling of the track had taken place. In the distance the line curves away towards the next station at Brookwood. It was quite a severe bend when taken at speed. Notice the neat garden between the two fast lines which has been reduced to a melancholy pile of spent ballast nowadays. (Lens of Sutton.)

SLIGHTLY OVER THE BORDER INTO SURREY for this view taken at Frimley Station on the LSWR route from Aldershot towards Ascot. The photograph was taken during the First World War and shows a detachment of soldiers alighting from a train complete with horse boxes. The salmon pink and brown livery of the rolling stock can be seen as a slight variation in the monochrome side of the coaches. (Lens of Sutton.)

A VIEW OF FLEET STATION between Farnborough and Basingstoke shortly after quadrupling. East of Basingstoke as far as Woking the design of the stopping places was similar, each serving what at the time was principally a rural community. Decades later Fleet is now one of a number of busy commuter stations that serves a large number of passengers going to Waterloo each working day. (Lens of Sutton.)

FLEET STATION seen from the opposite side with a London-bound express passing under the foot-bridge. The station buildings here were located at one end of the station for ease of access from the approach roads, although foresight provided for long platforms which would prove a boon in later years. (Lens of Sutton.)

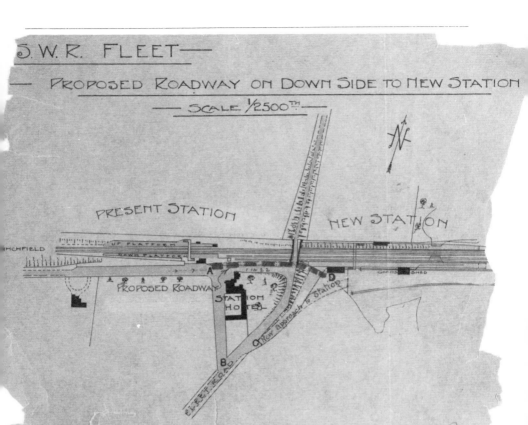

A PLAN OF FLEET showing the relative position of the new station compared with that of its predecessor.

WORK ON THE WIDENING OF THE LINE EASTWARDS towards Basingstoke took place around the turn of the century with completion in December 1904. The contractors J. Aird and Sons were responsible for the work, although, as seen here near Winchfield, matters did not go entirely to plan and problems occurred with a slip in the cutting side.

A CLOSE-UP OF THE FAILED CUTTING SIDE. Notice the primitive equipment available to the contractor on view at the top of the cutting. Today the evidence of such problems can still be seen in the gentle slopes of the bank at this point.

LARGEST OF ALL THE REBUILT STATIONS at this time was Basingstoke, shown here in one of a series of photographs taken shortly after the work was completed and showing the exterior of the 'down' side. Despite decades of change the exterior is largely unaltered today and presents a mellow brick façade in a town where concrete and glass are now prominent. (Lens of Sutton.)

BASINGSTOKE was one of the locations where the LSWR came into conflict with the GWR route from Reading – see p. 130. The result of this early competition was two separate stations side by side. This can just be seen in the photograph, with the GWR terminus and train shed on the right partly obscured by the telegraph poles. Despite rationalization its remains can still be seen today in the form of Platform 5 which the GWR used as the start and finish points for the diesel shuttle service from Reading to Basingstoke.

A PARTICULARLY INTERESTING VIEW of the LSWR station at Basingstoke, because the remains of the original stopping place are visible. This is identified by the shape of the platform canopy on the far left – now Platform 4 – with its characteristic droop and inclination. The structure survives to this day and is one of the few remaining canopies from the London and Southampton railway era. (Lens of Sutton.)

A WET AND SEEMINGLY EMPTY VIEW of the station taken from the west end and looking back towards London. Crossovers at either end of the station allowed trains access to one of two platforms in either direction, although it was the practice to route non-stop trains via the centre island platform. (Lens of Sutton.)

SEEN FOR THE FIRST TIME in this photograph is the Alton bay, playing host to what appears to be a solitary van. The railway was built on a slightly higher level than the surrounding ground, with the result that the platforms are level with the first floor of the station offices. This is clearly visible from the height of the houses on the extreme right. (Lens of Sutton.)

AN EARLY VIEW OF THE STATION with the GWR buildings on the right. Rebuilding would sweep away the original structure on the left which was designed by William Tite. The photograph was taken looking west towards Worting Junction. (Lens of Sutton.)

A FINAL VIEW OF THE STATION at Basingstoke showing what appears to be the shadow of the cameraman visible in the foreground. Notice what was a blue-on-white station name together with gas and oil lamps. (Lens of Sutton.)

BEING AN INTERCHANGE STATION, commodious facilities were provided at Basingstoke for the transhipment of goods. Indeed, the LSWR alone possessed both 'up' and 'down' goods yards, while the GWR had their own separate facilities. As a result, pilot and shunting duties were frequent between the various yards and it was a common sight to see vehicles from the other railway companies at the station.

APPROXIMATELY TWO MILES WEST of Basingstoke was Worting Junction and the point of divergence for the Bournemouth and Exeter routes. Originally a flat junction, a flyover was provided at the same time as the quadrupling from Woking took place, with work proceeding steadily at the time the photograph was taken. 'Up' trains from Bournemouth to London later used the flyover which is approached on a gradient of 1 in 106 from the south.

ALONE BETWEEN BASINGSTOKE AND WINCHESTER is the station at Micheldever, some two miles from the village of the same name. As a result a new development appropriately named Micheldever Station has grown up around the railway, and all because the landowners refused the original railway access to their lands. The photograph is looking north towards Basingstoke, with clean chalk to the right as evidence of where spoil has been removed for use in reclaiming land at Southampton. (Lens of Sutton.)

AS A RESULT OF MUCH CHALK REMOVAL at Micheldever a series of storage sidings was provided and used for stock awaiting entry to Eastleigh works. Today such facilities are no longer required and a new use for the area has emerged, in the form of a large petroleum storage and distribution depot. (Lens of Sutton.)

AN INFILTRATOR ON THE SCENE; GWR 43xx No. 4395 near Winchester Junction on a Portsmouth to Birmingham through train. Today the A34 link road passes underneath the railway near to where the photograph was taken.

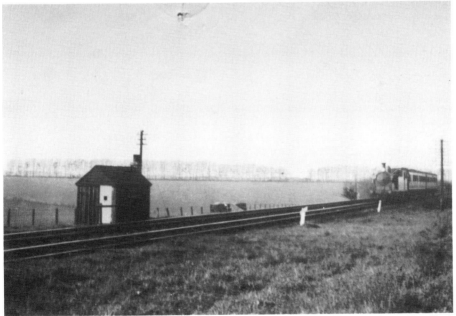

MOVING ON SOUTH TOWARDS WINCHESTER in the area known as Abbotts Barton. An unidentified '02' tank at the head of an Alton to Southampton train slowing for the stop at Winchester. (E. Branch.)

JUST NORTH OF WINCHESTER STATION a platform was provided in 1918 between the Andover Road and Park Road bridges for the use of Military traffic. This faded but extremely interesting view of the platform under construction, clearly shows the chalk which was cut away. Labour for this work was provided by men from a number of the nearby army camps including Flowerdown and Morn Hill. (Imperial War Museum.)

IN THIS VIEW the facilities are seen under construction. There was a separate connection in the far distance allowing trains direct access out onto the main line. (Imperial War Museum.)

Instructions to all concerned as to

Bringing into use a new Signal Box, between Winchester Junction and Winchester Station, to be known as "Winchester Loop," new and altered Signals in connection therewith, and a new Platform, on Wednesday, 4th December.

A new signal box, which will be known as "Winchester Loop," has been provided on the up line side, about 850 yards east of Winchester Station Box. It will communicate electrically with Winchester Junction on the one side and Winchester Station on the other.

The new signal box will be under the supervision of the Station Master at Winchester, and will be opened as required.

A crossover road, which will be worked from the new box, has been provided between the up and down lines opposite the signal box.

A facing connection, which will be worked from the new box, has been laid in from the down line to the down siding; the facing points in the down line are about 48 yards west of the signal box.

Catch points have been provided in the down siding at the fouling point with the facing connection.

A platform, 800 feet in length, has been constructed outside the down siding west of the new signal box.

The following are the new and altered signals:—

An up distant signal on the Winchester Station up starting signal post, 824 yards from the Winchester Loop up home signal.

An up home signal on the up line side, 37 yards west of the new signal box.

An up starting signal on the up line side, 417 yards east of the new signal box.

The Winchester Station down distant signal will also be the down distant signal for the new signal box, 962 yards from the Winchester Loop down home signal.

A two-arm post on the down line side, 34 yards east of the new signal box. See diagram:—

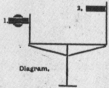

Diagram.

1. Winchester Loop down line to siding home signal.

2. Winchester Loop down main home signal.

A ground signal at the crossover road points in the up line controls movements from the up line to the siding.

A ground signal at the points in the siding controls movements from the siding to the up line.

A ground signal outside the siding at the fouling point of the crossing between the down line and down siding worked from Winchester Ground Frame "B" will control movements along the siding eastward.

The work will be in progress from 9.0 a.m. until completed on Wednesday, 4th December. **Mr. Barnes** to provide flagman, as required.

During the time the work is in progress drivers must look out for hand signals.

The District Inspector to be present when the altered signals, &c., are brought into use, and report to the District Superintendent on the working.

WATERLOO STATION,
29th November, 1918. (V. 31,809)

GEO. F. WEST,
Superintendent of the Line.

Waterlow & Sons Limited. Printers. London Wall, London.

EXTRACTS (this page and the next) from the official instructions relating to the introduction and later withdrawal of facilities at the Winchester (loop) troop platform. (Courtesy D. Cullum.)

LONDON & SOUTH WESTERN RAILWAY.

Instruction No. 6, 1920.

Instructions to all concerned as to the

ABOLITION OF WINCHESTER LOOP & BARNES BRIDGE SIGNAL BOXES & NEW & ALTERED SIGNALS, ETC.

ABOLITION OF WINCHESTER LOOP SIGNAL BOX.

(situate between Winchester Junction and Winchester Station).

On and from Sunday, 25th April.

Referring to Instruction No. 28, 1918, the Winchester Loop Signal Box will be abolished and the following signals, etc. removed :—

The crossover road between the up and down lines, situate opposite the signal box.

The facing connection from the down line to the down siding, situate 48 yards west of the signal box.

The catch points in the down siding, situate at the fouling point with the facing connection.

The up distant signal situate on the Winchester up starting signal post.

The up home, up starting, down main home and down line to siding home signals.

The ground signals, controlling movements to and from the up main line and the down siding.

The down distant signal for Winchester Loop and Winchester Station signal boxes will remain, but will in future apply to the latter section only.

The work will be in progress from 6.0 a.m. until completed, on Sunday, 25th April

Mr. BARNES to provide flagmen as required.

(A4/71,001).

AN UNUSUAL VIEW of the northern approach to Winchester station taken from Park Road overbridge. The train approaching the station is probably one from Alton. The van and coaches are stabled on what was the former troop platform and what is now referred to as the Baltic siding. Notice also the early colour light signal which was the 'up' distant signal for the worthy IBS. (E. Branch.)

SMOKE OVER WINCHESTER coinciding with storm clouds over Europe. A 'King Arthur' 4–6–0 No. 741 entering the station with a through train onto the GWR at Reading, 20 August 1939.

ALTHOUGH OF INDIFFERENT QUALITY, I could not resist the inclusion of this view of Winchester complete with a barrow load of luggage. (E. Branch.)

IN CONNECTION WITH the building of the Winchester by-pass during the 1930s a narrow gauge railway was laid by the contractor to assist in the removal of spoil from the workings. This can just be seen to the left of the view, while in the background is the GWR line through Winchester Chesil towards Newbury.

TWO FURTHER VIEWS OF THE WORKINGS in connection with the Winchester by-pass. They include the infamous iron bridge which is now the scene of almost continual traffic hold ups although, at the time the photograph was taken, singularly devoid of traffic. Notice the space either side of the abutments which allowed for the provision of an additional bridge to carry an extra line of rails if required at a later date. This was carried out on the 'down' side in 1943 when the 'down' loop line at Shawford was extended back as far as the DNS at Shawford Junction.

THE INTERIOR OF SHAWFORD JUNCTION SIGNAL BOX with its Westinghouse lever frame clearly visible. The box here was extended in 1931 when 'up' and 'down' loops were provided from Shawford to Allbrook. So, by means of suitable track circuits and electrically operated points and signals, the work of two other signal boxes, Shawford and Otterbourne, could be dispensed with.

A DELIGHTFUL VIEW north through Shawford station taken some time between 1919 and 1931. Visit the scene today and so much has changed. The crossovers between the 'up' and 'down' lines are gone, as are the connections from the goods yard. In addition, the signal box and station canopies are no more and a new 'down' relief line meanders its way around the back of the station. (Collection, Mrs Capon.)

OPENED IN 1841 to coincide with the branch to Gosport, Eastleigh must be one of the best known of all stations in Hampshire. Its façade remains basically unaltered to the present day and, although plans are now afoot for a major redesign of the facilities, they will, however, retain the Tite building. The photograph looks south along Southampton Road which has itself altered beyond recognition with none of the houses or shops seen in this view now remaining. (Lens of Sutton.)

CONVENIENTLY PLACED across the maze of sidings east of the station is the Bishopstoke Road bridge which has provided the vantage point for the photographer. This view shows the south yard with the carriage and wagon works to the left and the locomotive shops just visible in the distance. (Lens of Sutton.)

TO CATER FOR SIGHTING DIFFICULTIES occasioned by the station foot-bridge, the LSWR provided very tall signals for the 'up' line through the station with repeater arms just beneath. The arms themselves control the 'up' main, 'up' relief and Salisbury branch as well as the 'up' goods loop which ran parallel with the main lines as far north as Allbrook. The whole operation was controlled from Eastleigh East signal box, part of which is just visible on the extreme right. (J.R. Fairman.)

BUSY TIMES AT EASTLEIGH with luggage being dealt with on a 'down' train. In the background are some of the branches from the famous Eastleigh tree which has been a feature of Platforms 3 and 4 for many years.

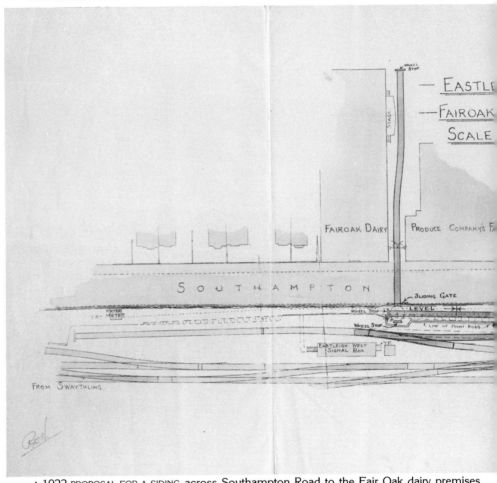

A 1922 PROPOSAL FOR A SIDING across Southampton Road to the Fair Oak dairy premises alongside the railway.

Scheme A.

Cancelled

E Co's Application. ———

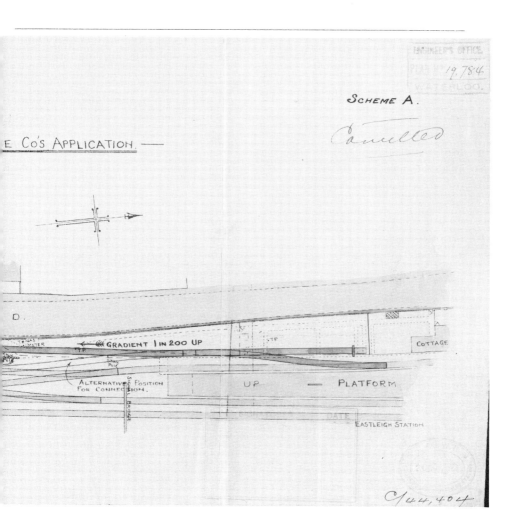

D.

← ≪ GRADIENT 1 IN 200 UP

STP

COTTAGE

ALTERNATIVE POSITION
FOR CONNECTION.

UP — PLATFORM

EASTLEIGH STATION

C/44,404

THIS TIME A PHOTOGRAPH TAKEN from the vantage point of the locomotive works' offices giving a panoramic view of the exits from the locomotive sheds on the left and the loco works on the right. Running left to right is the main Southampton railway, while the train on the extreme right is taking the line towards Botley and Fareham.

INSIDE THE LOCOMOTIVE WORKS with a boiler for a 'Lord Nelson' class engine clearly visible. Boiler work was one of the noisiest of all occupations in the workshop and yet there is no sign of any ear protection. Legislation to safeguard the welfare of the workers was still some years away.

A PROUD MOMENT for the works' rifle team, posed outside the offices with their challenge shield and cup.

TO CATER FOR THE INFLUX OF NEW WORKERS brought about by the establishment of the main running sheds and workshops at the town, the LSWR embarked on an ambitious programme of building residential accommodation. In this view houses are being erected in Campbell Road with the railway line a temporary affair provided to bring materials used in the construction.

MOVING SOUTH towards the next station of Swaythling. Originally there were plans to quadruple the line as far as Northam but these came to nothing, although the evidence in the form of the set back main building remains to this day. The station here was also built on a fairly sharp curve and would cause some difficulty to 'up' trains when restarting on a wet or greasy rail. (Lens of Sutton.)

SWAYTHLING IN EDWARDIAN DAYS with the delightful spectacle of a porter assisting some passengers to board a 'down' train. The station remains basically unaltered to this day, although the houses in the background have long since disappeared because of road improvements. (Lens of Sutton.)

TWO VIEWS OF ST DENYS STATION and the junction for the 'Netley road' from Southampton to Fareham. Trains for this route used the pair of platform faces to the extreme right. Some years before the Fareham line opened, a station called Portswood had existed near this site. It was closed in 1866 at the time the new route was opened. (Lens of Sutton.)

DESPITE YEARS OF SEARCHING no views have yet come to light of the extensive locomotive shed at Northam which closed at the turn of the century coinciding with the new depot at Eastleigh. In this recently found view, however, an 'M7' tank is depicted on the Northam depot turntable which afforded access to the shed roads. The group of men are more intent on having their photograph taken than completing the turning of the engine.

THE NORTHAM STATION PORTER proudly posed for the camera c. 1900. Northam was the last station before Southampton Terminus on the original railway. However, its importance diminished as a result of the opening of the curve to Southampton West and the line to Bournemouth. The actual junction can be seen beneath the overbridge which now carries the busy Northam Road traffic to and from the city. (Southampton University.)

OF PRIME IMPORTANCE to the railway at Southampton was the docks' traffic which consisted of both passenger and freight. Here a train load of cattle vans is seen crossing Canute Road, from alongside the Terminus station, into the docks themselves. The flagman is a very necessary precaution. (Southampton University.)

SHORTEST LIVED OF ALL THE PASSENGER SERVICES in the Southampton area was that serving the Royal Pier which operated for just 23 years from 1891 to 1914. Its demise came about officially because of the declaration of war, although competition from the street tramways would probably have forced it to curtail activities soon afterwards. (Lens of Sutton.)

A FURTHER VIEW OF THE RAILWAY and facilities on Southampton Royal Pier. Access to the little line was from the West or Blechynden station with through services direct from Waterloo which afforded ease of access onto the Isle of Wight ferry service which also started from this point. (Lens of Sutton.)

Southampton West. LSWR

STILL OPEN TODAY but now the only station to bear the name Southampton, this is the 'up' side exterior of the West station on the line to Bournemouth. Various rebuildings changed the appearance and size of the facilities from two very short platforms to a station which now has four long platform faces. Unfortunately the ornate clock tower is no longer visible having been demolished in 1967 at the time of the most recent reconstruction. (Lens of Sutton.)

FROM THE SOUTH SIDE THIS TIME with a group of men paused in their labours. Note also the two individuals up the telegraph pole. In connection with rebuilding and expansion in the 1930s this side of the station was swept away and replaced by two additional platform faces allied to a concrete station building in the garish style of the period. Other than necessary rebuilding following wartime bomb damage, it is the concrete station that survives today. (Lens of Sutton.)

Bottom, left.
SEEN HERE WITH TWO LONG PLATFORMS, this view of Southampton West is taken from the pedestrian foot-bridge spanning the lines. Behind the photographer was Southampton Tunnel which took the route to Northam and a connection into the main London line. Although not obvious from the photograph, there was a level crossing hard by the signal box.

A THROUGH SERVICE onto the GWR paused at the 'up' platform of Southampton West, the last vehicle of which appears to be a 40ft passenger brake van of late Victorian vintage. (Lens of Sutton.)

LOOKING TOWARDS LONDON through Southampton West station, this delightful view of 1911 portrays the facilities to advantage. The gentleman posed on the platform is presumably the station master. (W.E. Arden.)

A COMPANION TO THE PREVIOUS VIEW, this photograph provides a view of an amount of the station detail including the wind-breaks on the 'up' side. (W. E. Arden.)

SOME MILES WEST OF SOUTHAMPTON, in the heart of the picturesque New Forest, is Brockenhurst station, one of the more important stopping places on the line to Bournemouth. Here from 1888 was the point of divergence from the Bournemouth direct line via Sway. Brockenhurst had first become a junction four years earlier in 1884 with the opening of the short branch to Lymington. (Lens of Sutton.)

BUSY TIMES AT BROCKENHURST with the platforms full of activity. The lines in the centre are the main 'up' and 'down' platforms with the islands either side used both for the stopping services and the Brockenhurst–Lymington service. Notice also the different shape of the canopies. (Lens of Sutton.)

A VERY EARLY POSTCARD of the level crossing at Brockenhurst which allows the A337 Lymington road across the railway – the scene of considerable hold ups during the summer months. Years ago confusion arose over the naming of the station here and that of Brockenhurst on the Gosport line, the latter station being renamed Fort Brockhurst as a result. (Lens of Sutton.)

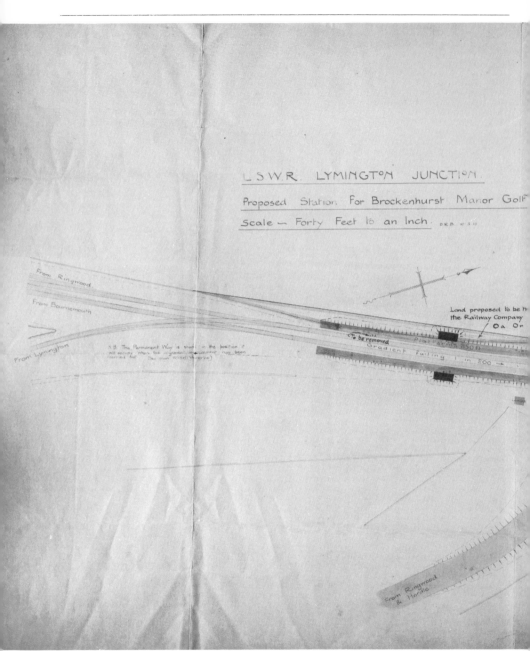

A FASCINATING DISCOVERY from 1913 for a halt at Lymington Junction. This was destined never to be built.

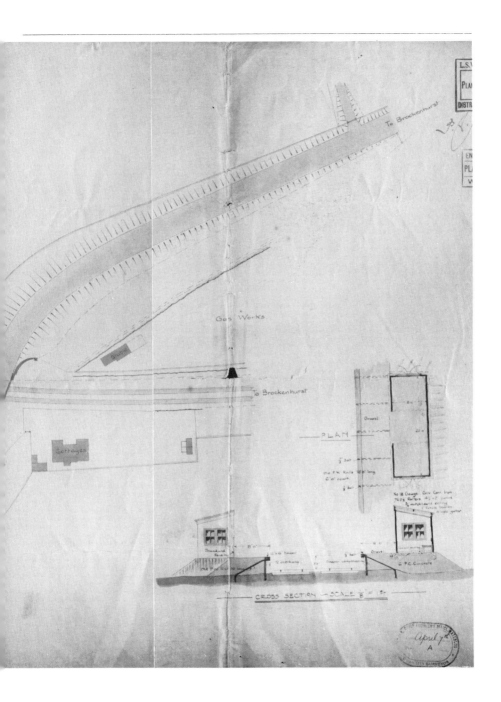

To Brockenhurst

Gas Works

To Brockenhurst

PLAN

Cottages

CROSS SECTION — SCALE 8 = 1 ft

53

A PANORAMIC VIEW OF THE STATION with part of the goods yard visible on the left. Further yards were provided on the opposite side of the line behind the camera. For a community the size of Brockenhurst the station was of considerable size, although traffic has developed over the years and it is now the railhead for much of the Forest area. (Lens of Sutton.)

THE BRANCH FROM BROCKENHURST TO LYMINGTON served the coastal town well and was destined to survive under electrification. As a result of its proximity to the foreshore, part of the route was carried on embankment and viaduct, both shown here with the town in the background. (Lens of Sutton.)

DESPITE ITS BARREN TERRAIN the Bournemouth direct line has often been the subject of various civil engineering difficulties, including here a serious embankment slip on the 'up' side of the line at Sway in 1949.

TYPICAL OF THE ARCHITECTURE FOR THE LESSER STATIONS on the Bournemouth direct line was the building at New Milton, with its wooden canopies and shelters fronting a brick station building. Notice also the twin-arch overbridge in the background, one of several on the route. (Lens of Sutton.)

TROOP MOVEMENTS at New Milton during the First World War. The regiment details are regretfully not recorded. (Lens of Sutton.)

BLANKETING WORK in progress at Hordle, near New Milton, in 1948 with the *Bournemouth Belle* cautiously passing the temporary signal box erected for the duration of the work.

Pokesdown. SR. 1931.

AS PART OF THE GENERAL IMPROVEMENT OF FACILITIES on the Southern during the early 1930s, the station at Pokesdown was completely rebuilt (this and the next five photographs). In place of the single island platform with wooden building, new platforms were erected either side a of four-track main line which, therefore, allowed a bypass for fast trains. (Lens of Sutton.)

Boscombe railway Station.

OPENED IN 1866, Boscombe station was the final stopping place before Bournemouth, although it has now been closed for some years. In happier times a Drummond 4–4–0 is seen at the head of an 'up' train, the first vehicle of which appears to be a four-wheeled van. (Lens of Sutton.)

BUILDING WORK AT BOURNEMOUTH CENTRAL STATION around the turn of the century. This was the only stopping place on the main line from Southampton to retain its overall roof into Southern days. It still survives today despite recent attempts to rationalize the facilities. (Lens of Sutton.)

THE EXTERIOR OF THE CENTRAL STATION at Bournemouth complete with its sumptuous façade. Bournemouth was a late developer as far as the railway network was concerned, although its popularity increased rapidly with the Victorian passion for bathing at favoured 'watering places'. (Lens of Sutton.)

BOURNEMOUTH STATION. — *Arrival of the London Train.* — I.

THE ARRIVAL OF THE LONDON TRAIN at Bournemouth. The fashions suggest that this was a seaside outing. (Lens of Sutton.)

72 BOURNEMOUTH. — The Central Station. — Interior. — LL.

INSIDE THE CENTRAL STATION. The two through lines were originally used either for stabling stock or the running of non-stop trains. Their importance diminished in later years when every passenger train was booked to call at the station. (Lens of Sutton.)

SERVING THE WESTERN EDGE OF THE TOWN was the West station at Bournemouth which was also the terminus for the trains from the joint Somerset and Dorset line from Bath. Unlike the Central station, this was a terminus with carriage berthing sidings nearby. (Lens of Sutton.)

THE NEXT SEVEN PICTURES SHOW the station at Bournemouth West which opened to traffic in 1874. It saw a life of just over 90 years before being considered redundant as a result of the Bournemouth electrification scheme. Among the trains originating from the station were the prestige *Bournemouth Belle* pullman service as well as the restaurant car portions of a number of the Weymouth line services. In addition, LMS engines from the Somerset and Dorset line were regular visitors which made the station a favourite for spotters during steam days. (Lens of Sutton.)

A RARE VIEW OF MEYRICK PARK HALT, situated between the two Bournemouth stations, which was opened on 1 March 1906. Principally served by the steam railmotor service, the stopping place was an early casualty of road competition and closed in October 1917. (Lens of Sutton.)

RETURNING NOW TO THE MAIN WEST OF ENGLAND LINE from Basingstoke towards Salisbury, this view of Overton station is typical of the wayside stopping places along the route. Note the siding full of wagons and the ornate barge-boarding to the end of the station building. (Lens of Sutton.)

FOUR VIEWS OF ANDOVER JUNCTION STATION showing the facilities to advantage. The track layout here allowed a refuge to slower trains while the station was the junction for the MSWJ route north towards Swindon and Cheltenham and also the 'Sprat and Winkle' line south to Ramsey and Southampton. (Lens of Sutton.)

Great Snowstorm in Andover. Junction Station

RAILWAY SMASH AT ANDOVER
FRED.WRIGHT
ANDOVER

THE AFTERMATH OF THE ANDOVER RAILWAY CRASH in 1914. The driver over-ran the signals with the result that his train collided with the rear of a number of stationary livestock wagons. Fortunately there were no serious human casualties.

A DELIGHTFUL VIEW OF PETERSFIELD STATION on the Portsmouth direct line which was opened to traffic in 1859. Five years later the station became the junction for the little branch to Midhurst and a meeting with the rival LBSCR company. Despite attempts to the contrary, Petersfield would remain in LSWR hands for the life of the company.

OPENED IN JUNE 1933 to serve the adjacent racecourse, Paulsgrove Halt, between Cosham and Porchester, saw a limited amount of traffic before ceasing to be used after 1939. It was destined never to re-open. (Lens of Sutton.)

STAFF GROUPED AROUND A DIMINUTIVE 'C14' 2–2–0 motor tank at Cosham. This was one of a class of ten similar engines built at Nine Elms between 1906 and 1909 at a cost of just £910 each. They were intended to supplement the early steam railmotors but proved incapable of the tasks required and so a number were graduated to shunting duties and later rebuilt with the 0–4–0T wheel arrangement. No. 745 is here depicted at Cosham sometime prior to 1913.

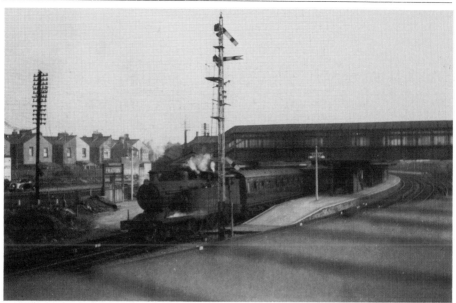

REFERRED TO AT TIMES AS FRATTON OR FRATTON & SOUTHSEA STATION, this was the final stopping place before the main line reached Portsmouth. The confusion in names was partly due to the short-lived East Southsea branch (see later photographs), whose trains departed from their own separate platforms. (Lens of Sutton.)

82

THE EFFECTS OF ENEMY ACTION on the locomotive shed at Fratton. Despite considerable damage the object of the raid was not achieved and all the engines were repaired.

THE BRANCH PLATFORMS at Fratton for the East Southsea service in use from 1885 to 1914. Today the site of the branch platforms is occupied by an EMU servicing depot, although the foot-bridge still remains, albeit devoid of its overall covering. (Lens of Sutton.)

STEAM RAILMOTOR NO. 1 stored alongside Fratton shed — note the solid wheels. The breakdown crane and wagons are also of interest and present a somewhat Dickensian appearance, though adequate for the time. Fratton was a joint station with the LBSCR who operated the coast route from Brighton and, as a result, there were in fact two separate sheds side by side. Each would continue its independent operation until forced to amalgamate under the grouping of railways in 1923. (National Railway Museum.)

ALTHOUGH OF INDIFFERENT QUALITY this view of a train on the East Southsea branch is of particular interest. Views of this little line are rare and yet here is a Fratton to Southsea service, probably in the days prior to 1900. The open space either side of the tracks is now the subject of urban development. (Collection, John Minnis.)

ANOTHER RARE FIND, this time of Albert Road, one of the two Halts on the East Southsea branch. This and the other halt at Jessie Road were opened in an attempt to combat competition from the street tramways and coincided with the service being operated by steam railmotors on just one of the running lines. This explains why there is a platform on only one side of the line. (National Railway Museum.)

A REMARKABLE PHOTOGRAPH of the terminus at East Southsea showing, on the left, the extension to the new terminus close to Granada Road. The large facilities of the old station are also visible, intended for a traffic that was never to materialize. In the platform the coaches are probably stabled stock. The East Southsea was a jointly operated branch between the LSWR and the LBSCR, this giving rise to the peculiar arrangement whereby each company operated the service for alternate years, providing their own staff only during the time they were responsible for the trains. (National Railway Museum.)

A CHARACTERISTIC OF SO MANY EARLY RAILWAY PHOTOGRAPHS is the delightful way in which the staff were prepared to be photographed while performing their everyday duties. Here the crew of the engine are posed with members of the Hampshire Regiment on their way to camp from Portsmouth Town station. (Lens of Sutton.)

BUSY TIMES in the yards adjacent to Portsmouth Town station. Shunting in the yard is a 'G6' 0–6–0T engine, while just visible in the background is the ramp taking the passenger lines to their final destination at Portsmouth harbour station. (Lens of Sutton.)

THE EFFECTS OF AN AIR RAID at Portsmouth Town station in the spring of 1941. The railwayman is seen surveying the damage of what was to be a frequent target for the enemy. (Southern Railway).

DAMAGED COACHING STOCK at Portsmouth in 1941. (Southern Railway.)

THE EFFECTS OF AN EARLIER RAID on the Harbour station in August 1940. The twisted metal stanchions, charred timbers and damaged crane are a gaunt reminder of a foul deed. (Southern Railway.)

SEEN FROM THE AIR the effects of enemy action are more pronounced and the various bomb sites and damaged buildings are readily apparent. The railway itself sweeps south from Fratton on the extreme left before either entering the town station or continuing off to the right towards the harbour. Notice also the dockyard branch which diverges off the main line and curves towards the bottom centre of the photograph. (Southern Railway.)

REBUILDING AND REMODELLING WORK at Havant station in 1937/8. Just behind the photographer was the junction for the lines to Brighton and Petersfield, while the Hayling Island branch also ran into the station from its route on the extreme left-hand side.

A FORMER BRIGHTON 'TERRIER' TANK receiving attention at Havant station. The Hayling Island branch was worked exclusively by this class of engine, a number of which were stabled at Fratton for the purpose. The disc with the number '372' relates to the duty number applicable to the engine crews working. (Lens of Sutton.)

THE TERMINUS AT HAYLING ISLAND, just a very short walk from the beach. Here in summertime trains swollen with trippers would arrive, though, at the opposite extreme, the winter services were sparsely patronized. (Lens of Sutton.)

WICKHAM was one of five intermediate stations on the former Meon Valley line from Alton to Fareham and is shown here when brand new in 1903. The extensive buildings provided accommodation for both the railway passenger and the station master and family, and were intended to provide for a wealth of traffic that never materialized.

THE DELIGHTFULLY NAMED STATION AT PRIVETT on the Meon Valley line seen here to advantage, looking almost like a country house. Unlike Wickham, Privett still survives today, although it is many years since a train ran between its platforms. (Collection, Ray Bartlett.)

DROXFORD STATION probably shown when brand new. The foot-bridge was typical of those provided on the railway. A number of these had a short life, being demolished in a freak blizzard which swept the Hampshire countryside in the winter of 1927. The view is looking north towards West Meon. (Lens of Sutton.)

A CHARMING PAIR OF VIEWS showing some of the navvies engaged in the construction of the Meon Valley line at the turn of the century. Responsible for the building of the line were Messrs Robert T. Relf & Son who, besides working with human power, also engaged the services of at least eight small steam engines as well as various cranes and excavators. (Courtesy John King.)

LOOKING NORTH THROUGH WICKHAM STATION towards Droxford. Despite being laid out with speed and main-line traffic in mind, the Meon Valley route was never anything more than a branch, although its double-track earthworks still remain in silent tribute to trains that no longer pass. Perhaps typifying the lack of traffic, this photograph does well to illustrate the quiet nature of the line – an intended main route and yet allowing time for conversation upon the platform. (Lens of Sutton.)

A PHOTOGRAPH purported to have been taken either at, or very soon after, the opening, this is also Wickham with an Adams 4–4–2 'Radial' tank at the head of a train bound for Fareham. (Lens of Sutton.)

POSTMARKED 18 September 1903, this particular card of Wickham is addressed to a Miss D. Kent of Southsea and states: 'The picture on the other side is one of the sites – E.G.K.' One of a number of cards bearing similar messages and posted from the line around this time.

The Viaduct, Westmeon   Emm's Series

IN ORDER TO CROSS THE DOWNLAND OF HAMPSHIRE the Meon Valley line involved considerable earthworks and features of civil engineering which included two tunnels as well as this viaduct at West Meon. Necessary repairs to the structure were one of the points which contributed towards closure of the line in 1955. Other than a concrete stump, no traces of the viaduct now remain. (Collection, Ray Bartlett.)

THREE CHANCE FINDS OF PRIVETT STATION believed to have been taken around the early 1920s. This was a time when economies were already dictated for the Meon Valley route and Privett was one of the stations destined to lose the use of its passing loop and signal box. (Collection, Ray Bartlett.)

FOR MANY YEARS the transport of soft fruit by train was an important business in south Hampshire for the LSWR and its successor, the Southern Railway. The short fruit season saw a rush of traffic as the growers attempted to get their produce to market in the shortest time. Botley, on the line between Eastleigh and Fareham, was one of the locations used as a railhead and the photograph shows the otherwise quiet station transformed albeit as a temporary measure. (Lens of Sutton.)

Botley Station.

THE STATION APPROACH TO BOTLEY which was from the road leading to Swanmore and Bishop's Waltham. The station buildings are on the right-hand side, while the alternative forms of transport, horse and car, make for an interesting comparison. (Lens of Sutton.)

BOTLEY was also the junction for the little branch to Bishop's Waltham which for some years was operated by a steam railmotor service. Today it is almost 50 years since a regular passenger train used the bay platform seen here and yet the track remains as a headshunt and siding for the stone trains which use Botley as a discharge terminal. (Lens of Sutton.)

THE TERMINUS AT BISHOP'S WALTHAM with its ornate tile-hung buildings, possibly unique among the station buildings of Hampshire. Today the site of the railway is hard to visualize, having disappeared under a roundabout and new road scheme. However, just south of the station the trackbed has been converted into a public footpath. (Lens of Sutton.)

FAREHAM STATION possesses a chequered past, being first on the branch line to Gosport and later overtaken in importance by the Portsmouth line running via Cosham. Accordingly, the track layout of the station is very much an *ad hoc* affair abounding with sharp curves and the associated speed restrictions which are all a throw back to the early years of railway construction in the county. (Lens of Sutton.)

A CHANCE FIND at a postcard fair turned up this rare view of the short-lived Stokes Bay line at Little Anglesey near Gosport. Intended as an important part of the quickest route to the Isle of Wight via Stokes Bay, the line was effectively stifled by the competition between the LSWR and LBSCR companies. This meant that the railway failed to capitalize on what could well have been a great commercial success.

Bottom, left.
ONE OF THE MOST ORNATE OF ALL THE STATIONS in the county was at Gosport. Unfortunately it is seen here from the track side and so the famous colonnade is invisible. The decline of Gosport station began almost as soon as it was opened, for the military garrison refused the railway access to the waterfront and so its importance as a railhead for Portsmouth was seriously in doubt. Later on, air raids woud all but destroy the station while a mediocre service of passenger trains did little to boost trade. Accordingly passenger services were withdrawn in 1953 and Gosport had for many years the distinction of being the largest town in England devoid of railway communication. The train seen is bound for Fareham with a 'Brighton Tank' at its head. (Lens of Sutton.)

L.
ANGLESE
Diagra

STOKES BAY UP STARTING SIGNAL

431 YARDS   110 YARDS   CROSSING

SLOTTED FROM STOKES
BAY TO FORM UP ADVANCE
STARTING SIGNAL

BAY
CROSSING   A

FROM STOKES BAY

STOKES
LEVEL   A   GATEMANS
BOX

LEVER IN GATEMANS
BOX CONTROLS
WICKETS AT "A" "A"

ANGLESEA LEVEL

CROSSING

91 YARDS

FALLS→1IN290\
FOR 120YARDS   LEVEL FOR 231 YDS   GRADIENTS   FALLS→

Mechani

Nos	DESCRIPTION
1	UP DISTANT SIGNAL
2	UP HOME SIGNAL
3	UP STARTING SIGNAL
4	STOKES BAY CROSSING GATE LOCK
5	ANGLESEA CROSSING WICKETS
6	ANGLESEA CROSSING GATE LOCK
7	SIDING POINTS
8 PULL	FROM SIDING DISC
8 PUSH	TO SIDING DISC
9	DOWN STARTING SIGNAL
10	DOWN HOME SIGNAL
11	DOWN DISTANT SIGNAL
12	ST MARKS LANE CROSSING WICKETS

WITH A SINGULAR LACK OF PHOTOGRAPHIC VIEWS of the Stokes Bay line it is necessary to make recourse to official documents. The signalling plans provide a good idea of the track layout along part of the route. (British Railways.)

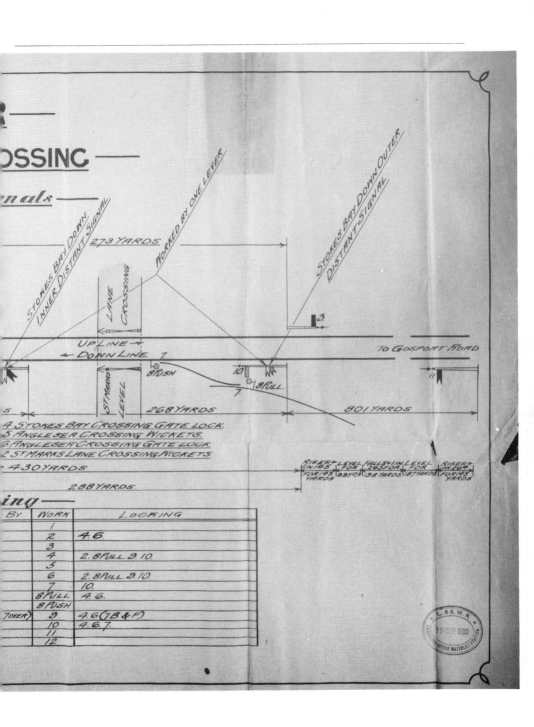

R———

OSSING———

nals———

STOKES BAY DOWN INNER DISTANT SIGNAL

273 YARDS

WORKED BY ONE LEVER

LANE CROSSING

STOKES BAY DOWN OUTER DISTANT SIGNAL

3

UP LINE →
← DOWN LINE 7

TO GOSPORT ROAD

ST MARKS LEVEL

8 PUSH

10

W

8 PULL.

7

11

S

268 YARDS

801 YARDS

4 STOKES BAY CROSSING GATE LOCK.
5 ANGLESEA CROSSING WICKETS.
6 ANGLESEA CROSSING GATE LOCK.
2 ST MARKS LANE CROSSING WICKETS

430 YARDS

288 YARDS

RISES+ LEVEL FALLS IN LEVEL RISES+
IN 145 FOR 265 FOR IN 264
FOR 145 99 YDS. 98 YARDS 187 YARDS FOR 145
YARDS YARDS

ing———

	BY	WORK	LOCKING
		1	
		2	4.6.
		3	
		4	2.8 PULL. 9. 10.
		5	
		6	2.8 PULL. 9. 10.
		7	10.
		8 PULL	4.6.
		8 PUSH	
	(OVER)	9	4.6 (1B & F)
		10	4.6.7.
		11	
		12	

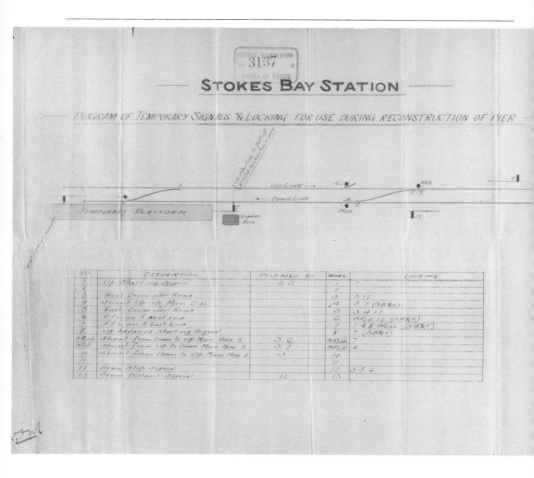

STOKES BAY STATION

Diagram of Temporary Signals & Locking for use during Reconstruction of Pier

No.	Description	Released by	Work	Locking
1	Up Starting Signal	G B	1	7
2			2	
3	West Cross over Road		3	5 12
4	Shunt Up Up Main O.S.s		4	5 7 (SBXF)
5	East Cross over Road		5	3 4 12
6	F.P.L. on 5 West End		6	9 Fob. 12 (SBXF)
7	F.P.L. on 5 East End		7	1 4 8 9Rob. (SBXF)
8	Up Advance Starting Signal		8	7 (SBXF)
9 Rob.	Shunt from Down to Up Main thro 5	5 6	9 Rob.	7
9 R.oll.	Shunt from Up to Down Main thro 5	5 7	9 R.oll.	3
10	Shunt from Down to Up Main thro 3	3	10	
11			11	
12	Down Stop Signal		12	3 5 6
13	Down Distant Signal	12	13	

IT WAS ALMOST AS IF THE GOSPORT PENINSULA was the haunt of the most obscure of railways for, diverging at Fort Brockhurst was the little Lee-on-the-Solent line which was built with great hopes for the development of the watering place it served. This early view of a Lee line train shows the primitive accommodation then provided to lesser line services of the period. (Lens of Sutton.)

THERE WERE SEVERAL HALTS on the short line to Lee, most of which possessed level crossings, which seemed to accrue more than their fair share of altercations between train and car! Of particular interest in this early view of Browndown Halt is the use of concrete as the basic building material. This is a substance that would later be used with considerable effect throughout the LSWR and SR systems. (Lens of Sutton.)

TRIPPERS enjoying their visit to the beach at Lee-on-the-Solent. The terminus of the railway can just be seen in the background, the proximity to the beach being obvious. Today, the main station buildings survive but they have been converted into an amusement arcade. A line of beach huts occupies the spot where trains used to stand. (Lens of Sutton.)

CHANDLERS FORD STATION on the original line west from Eastleigh to Salisbury. The line through here lost its passenger service some years ago and has been singled, although it remains an important diversionary link between Eastleigh and Salisbury.

A GATHERING OF STATION STAFF AND OTHERS at Romsey, although quite what the celebration was is not recorded. Behind the group the variety of advertising posters make for interesting reading and include one for the department store of Tyrell & Green which is still extant in Southampton. (Lens of Sutton.)

BUILT FOR PART OF ITS LENGTH along the former canal, the line from Redbridge through Romsey towards Andover has had a colourful and eventful history. Suffice it to say that it was almost the means for the GWR to gain a foothold in Southampton, although this was denied them at the eleventh hour. Nursling station has regretfully been closed for a number of years, although the rails still pass the site on the southern section of the line between Redbridge and Romsey. (Lens of Sutton.)

DEAN STATION west of Romsey and on the way to Salisbury. Compare this with the later view in the companion volume *Wiltshire Railways in Old Photographs* and the changes brought about over the years are apparent. For example the signal box shown here is in probably near original condition with its exposed cross timbers which were later shrouded from view with matchboarding. (Lens of Sutton.)

STORED AWAITING THEIR FATE, a line-up of perhaps 30 engines wait for the call to Eastleigh Works from the sidings at Kimbridge just west of Romsey. A number of otherwise life-expired steam engines were retained for use during the 1940s. With the return of peace it took some time to catch up with the backlog of repairs and scrappings. Most of those shown here were truely beyond reprieve and were to be called to the scrapyard. (Lens of Sutton.)

ANDOVER CANAL RAILWAY.

CAPITAL, £130,000; IN 13,000 SHARES OF £10 EACH.

DEPOSIT, £1 PER SHARE,

PURSUANT TO THE STANDING ORDERS OF PARLIAMENT.

(The liability of the Shareholders will be limited by the Act to the amount of their Shares.)

PROVISIONAL DIRECTORS.

THOMAS HEARD MORTIMORE, Esq. -	Mayor of Andover.
WILLIAM CUBITT, Esq. M.P. -	Penton Lodge, Andover.
RALPH ETWALL, Esq. -	Andover.
THOMAS EDWARDS, Esq. -	Compton House, Stockbridge.
WILLIAM BUNCE GREENFIELD, Esq.	Portchester Terrace, North Hyde Park.
GEORGE HUNT, Esq. -	Southampton.
HOWARD JOHN KENNARD, Esq. -	54, Cleveland Square, Hyde Park
JOHN RAVENHILL, Esq. -	Warminster.
J. R. STEBBING, Esq. -	Southampton.
HENRY THOMPSON, Esq. -	Andover.

(WITH POWER TO ADD TO THEIR NUMBER.)

BANKERS.

THE HAMPSHIRE BANKING COMPANY.
MESSRS. HEATH, Andover.

ENGINEER.

J. S. BURKE, Esq.

SOLICITORS.

THOMAS LAMB, Esq. Andover.
MESSRS. DEACON, STEAD and TYLEE, Southampton.
W. T. MANNING, Esq. 20, Great George Street, Westminster.

PROSPECTUS.

The object proposed by this undertaking is the conversion of the Andover Canal throughout its entire course, from Andover through Stockbridge and Romsey to Redbridge, a length of about twenty-two miles, into a Railway.

The proposed line will shorten the distance between Southampton and Andover, as compared with the present circuitous Railway route, by nearly one half, whilst it will afford to Stockbridge and the fertile Valley of the Test, the benefits of Railway Communication, from which they are at present wholly shut out, and it will also lessen the distance between Southampton and Romsey by about one fourth.

Arrangements have been made, consequent on the recent opening of the Devizes branch of the Great Western Railway, which will ensure the completion of the Devizes and Hungerford line, and by the construction of fourteen miles of additional Railway from Andover to the neighbourhood of Pewsey, to join such last mentioned line, a direct communication from Southampton to Bristol and South Wales will be opened, which will be only about Two miles longer than the existing route by way of Salisbury. By continuing the proposed line from Redbridge, across the Mud Lands to the Western Shore, an independent Terminus into Southampton, which has been so long desired, will be obtained.

The Canal is singularly adapted for the construction of a cheap line of Railway. There will be no Tunnel or Viaduct, and the works will be of the most inexpensive character. The Landowners are most favourable to the undertaking, being very desirous of having a Railway substituted for the Canal, and as the Canal Company are in possession of the district, there can be no reason to doubt that the line (which is similar to that for which the South Western Railway Company, in the year 1847, obtained powers, but failed to construct) will receive the sanction of Parliament. The entire absence of Engineering difficulties, and the extremely low cost of construction, fully justify the expectation that the line will be remunerative to the Shareholders.

As regards the traffic, the safest data are the returns of the existing lines of Railway. On five only of the English lines is the weekly traffic below £20 per mile, whilst the average of all the Railways of the United Kingdom is about £47 per mile per week.

Assuming the receipts on the projected line to be only £20 per mile
per week, the total per annum would amount to .. £22,880
Deduct, say £50 per cent., for working expenses £11,440

Leaving applicable for Dividend £11,440

The Canal Company have agreed to take a considerable portion of their purchase money in Shares of the Railway Company.

The necessary Plans have been lodged, notices given, and other Deposits made up to the 31st December to enable the Provisional Directors to apply to Parliament for an Act in the present Session.

Applications in the accompanying Form for the remaining Shares may be made to the Solicitors.

HORSEBRIDGE STATION on the northern half of the Andover to Redbridge route, although in the best traditions of railway namings King's Somborne would probably have been more accurate. The station is typical of the rural stopping places on the line which meandered gently through the Test valley and which could expect little traffic other than that associated with a primarily rural community. (Lens of Sutton and Author's collection.)

MOST IMPORTANT OF ALL THE STOPPING PLACES north of Romsey was at Stockbridge, a pleasant small market town famed for its wide High Street and Georgian style shops. Into this community the railway was very much an intruder and although it served the area well for a number of years it is not surprising to relate how, with closure, all traces have now been removed and the town has reverted to a quiet charm similar to that of the last century. (Lens of Sutton.)

RAILWAY STATION. STOCKBRIDGE.

THE LARGEST OF ALL THE STATIONS on the line north of Romsey was at Fullerton, which became a junction in consequence of the opening of the connecting line from Hurstbourne in 1885. Originally called Fullerton Bridge the old stopping place was resited due to the intrusion of the new line and yet it is the new station that has today been demolished with the old converted into a private residence. (Lens of Sutton.)

CLATFORD STATION south of Andover which served a number of villages dotted around the area. (Lens of Sutton.)

ANDOVER TOWN STATION (this and the next two photographs) was conveniently placed in the middle of the shopping centre. Unfortunately heavy motor traffic caused considerable hold-ups at the level crossing visible at the end of the platform which, no doubt, contributed towards the line's eventual closure. Today the site had been cleared and all traces of the railway have disappeared under an urban rebuilding scheme. (Lens of Sutton.)

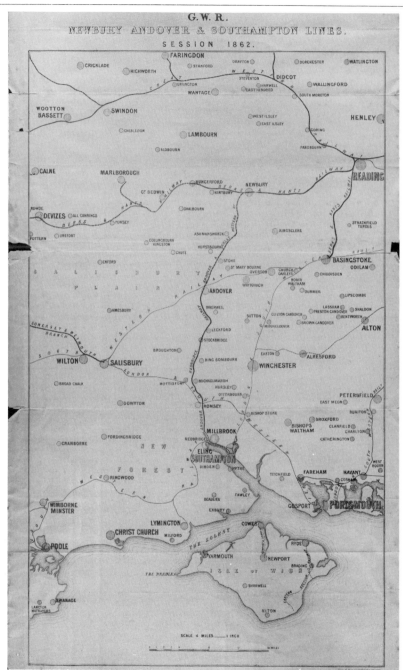

PROPOSAL MAP for a railway that was never built between Newbury and Andover, which also gives an idea as to the intentions of the GWR in reaching Southampton.

RETURNING AGAIN TO FULLERTON JUNCTION, this time for a pictorial trip along the 'Nile Valley' towards Hurstbourne. The intrusion of the new line almost meant two stations alongside each other with the Hurstbourne line diverging to the right. Notice the pedestrian on the right-hand side who appears to be having some difficulty in controlling his dog! (Lens of Sutton.)

TRAFFIC BETWEEN HURSTBOURNE AND FULLERTON was always very small. Indeed, this was the price the LSWR had to pay for building the line at all – a vain and failed attempt to prevent the DN & S route passing south of Whitchurch. Accordingly this view of No. 614 attached to a solitary coach is typical of the traffic in later years and it is not surprising to relate that the line closed very early on. (Lens of Sutton.)

THREE DELIGHTFUL VIEWS of Wherwell station near Fullerton, pronounced locally as 'Whirl'. The importance given to the little railway is obvious with its double track layout and extensive facilities that are more reminiscent of an intended main line. The scenery along the line was also said to be magnificent, although this first part of the route traversed a deep chalk cutting. Queen Victoria is said to have travelled the route on several occasions and likened its views to that alongside the Nile in Egypt. No doubt this is how the route obtained its peculiar nickname of 'Nile Valley'. (Lens of Sutton and Author's collection.)

INSIDE THE GREAT WESTERN STATION at Basingstoke. A rare view underneath the cavernous interior of a train shed typical of so many GWR lines. In the distance the line continues as a shunting spur towards one of the LSWR goods yards, while across the running lines is a baggage way used to connect the two platforms. (Lens of Sutton.)

GWR 4–4–0 NO. 3556 approaching Basingstoke from Reading and passing the GWR signal box – later redesignated 'Basingstoke C'. Passing from left to right are the connections onto the LSWR system which were subsequently straightened out to afford an easier connection between the two companies. (Lens of Sutton.)

THE GWR ORIGINS OF MORTIMER STATION on the route between Basingstoke and Reading are obvious from this view with the wide gap between the running lines an indication that this was originally a broad gauge route. Today the platforms have been extended widthways, and the baulk track has disappeared to be replaced by conventional fittings. Notice also the well laid out station gardens which won several prizes in the company's station gardens competition. Ironically, despite having been under Southern Region control for many years, Mortimer is probably the last of the masonry-built wayside stations designed during Brunel's time and, as such, is secure as a listed building. (Lens of Sutton.)

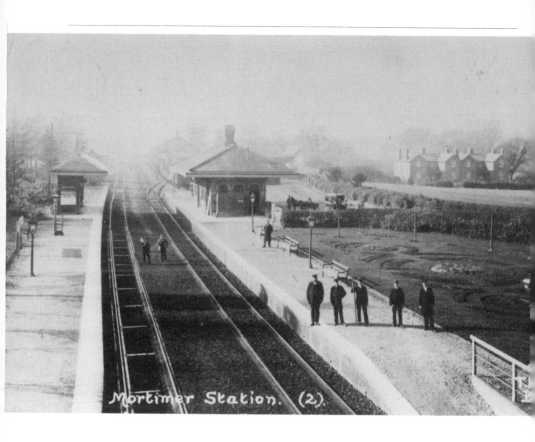

Mortimer Station. (2).

Bottom, right.
NOW A SUBURB OF SOUTHAMPTON, the station at Bitterne, on the line from St Denys to Fareham, gives the impression of being a rural stopping place. Bearing in mind the considerable motor-vehicle congestion around the area at peak times, it is perhaps surprising that more use is not made of the service into the centre of Southampton. However, with a variety of suggestions in the area for 'rapid transit systems' the railway may once again see a revival of its fortunes. (Lens of Sutton.)

NO LOOK AT THE LINES IN HAMPSHIRE would be complete without a brief glance at the Basingstoke and Alton route. Another obscure railway and one on which there is a considerable photographic shortfall. Suffice it to say that the B & A was, in every sense, a light railway which had the distinction (or indignity) of being closed during the First World War in order for its trackwork to be taken up for use elsewhere. Despite attempts by the SR to quietly forget the line a legal loophole ensured the railway was relaid although, as seen here, with only the barest minimum of facilities. In this new guise its life was short and it closed in the 1930s. (Lens of Sutton.)

A CHARACTERISTIC OF THE NETLEY ROUTE was the way it followed the course of the foreshore for the early part of its way east from Southampton, and as a result it abounds in reverse curves. They are clearly seen at Woolston station in these views looking back towards Southampton. Today the main buildings and signal box still remain – the latter in private hands, although the goods yard site has been redeveloped for private housing. (Lens of Sutton.)

CURRENTLY ENJOYING A REVIVAL IN POPULARITY is the country park at Netley, just east of Southampton, although a far cry from its origins as the grounds surrounding a military hospital. To serve the sanatorium a short railway was laid through the grounds from the main line at Netley station. Here an LSWR 'M7' 0–4–4T is coupled next to an ambulance coach alongside the special hospital platform. (Lens of Sutton.)

THE QUAINT FACILITIES of the original Bursledon station situated next to the famous Hamble river. The line was later doubled through here and now forms an important section of the route traversed by the direct services which operate between Portsmouth and Cardiff. (Lens of Sutton.)

ALRESFORD STATION on the Mid-Hants route from Winchester to Alton; now the headquarters of the preserved Watercress line. (Lens of Sutton.)

THE LOVELY RURAL SETTING of Ropley station north of Alresford, seen here with its original passing loop and signal box before both were swept away under the economies of 1931. Subsequently the station consisted of a single platform face and small yard, access to which was via a ground frame locked by the single line tablet. (Lens of Sutton.)

LONDON AND SOUTH-WESTERN RAILWAY.

Board of Trade (Railway Department),
8, Richmond Terrace, Whitehall, London, S.W.
January 21st, 1901.

SIR,

I HAVE the honour to report, for the information of the Board of Trade, in compliance with the Order of the 2nd instant, the result of my enquiry into the causes of the collision which occurred on the 27th December, about 5.10 p.m., near Ropley, on the London and South-Western Railway.

In this case, the 2.45 p.m. passenger train from Waterloo to Southampton, on arrival at Medstead Station, had to detach its last vehicle, a horse box. After this was done and the train had started towards Ropley, the next station, the horse box took charge, and following the train down the incline, collided with the rear brake van at a point about 300 yards beyond Ropley Station.

The collision was fortunately not a violent one, and only five passengers complained of having been shaken.

One pair of wheels of the horse box was derailed, and the buffers of the box and brake van were locked and damaged, but the horse appears not to have been injured.

No damage was done to the permanent way.

8636   M 2

92

Description.

The scene of this accident is on the single line branch of the London and South-Western Railway, between Farnham and Winchester. The railway runs, generally speaking, in a north-east and south-west direction, and has not much curvature. The north-east end of Medstead Station is the highest point on this line. From this point the line falls towards Alton Station in the up direction at an inclination of 1 in 60, for a distance of about $3\frac{1}{4}$ miles. To the south-west also, the line falls through Medstead Station at 1 in 200 for about 350 yards. Then follow falling gradients of 1 in 60, and 1 in 80, which have lengths respectively of about $2\frac{1}{4}$ and $2\frac{1}{2}$ miles. Through Ropley Station, a little more than 3 miles from Medstead, a falling gradient of 1 in 250, with a length of about 300 yards, occurs.

The arrangements at Medstead and Ropley stations are generally similar. In each case there is a loop from 250 to 350 yards in length, and a siding. In the case of Medstead, the siding is situated at the south-west end of the station, and is connected with the up loop line. At Ropley, however, the siding is at the north-west end of the station, and forms a junction with the down loop line. In both cases the points trail to trains travelling in the proper direction.

On the day in question, the train, after discharging passengers at Medstead Station on the down platform, drew ahead on to the single line clear of the loop points. It was then set back far enough on the up loop line to allow the horse box to be detached at the up platform, at a spot a few yards beyond the points giving access to the siding. These points face a vehicle entering the siding, and lie normally for the main line and not for the siding. The horse box was thus detached on a gradient falling towards Ropley of 1 in 200. About 25 yards in the direction of Ropley, from the point where the horse box was uncoupled, the falling gradient changed to 1 in 60.

The horse box was, unlike the remainder of the train, the property of the Midland and South-Western Junction Railway Company, and had solid wheels. It was fitted with the vacuum brake pipe, but not with a hand brake.

MEDSTEAD STATION — later Medstead and Four Marks — the final station before reaching Alton. The railway approached the site here via a stiff climb from both sides and, as a result, it was the practice to double-head heavy trains throughout the course of the Mid-Hants line. (Lens of Sutton.)

ALDERSHOT STATION (this and the next two photographs) dealt with an amount of military traffic. Notice the commodious facilities, particularly for goods, while the flying of the flags and bunting could well indicate the return of a particular regiment to its home depot. (Lens of Sutton.)

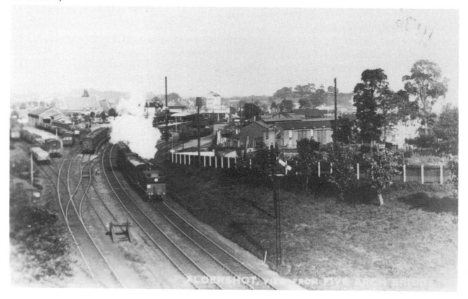

SITUATED ON THE ORIGINAL LINE WEST from Southampton towards Wimborne and Dorchester, Ringwood station declined in importance with the opening of the Bournemouth direct route. Even so, it was a useful diversionary route as well as being the junction for the original line to Bournemouth from the east which served Hurn and Christchurch. (Lens of Sutton.)

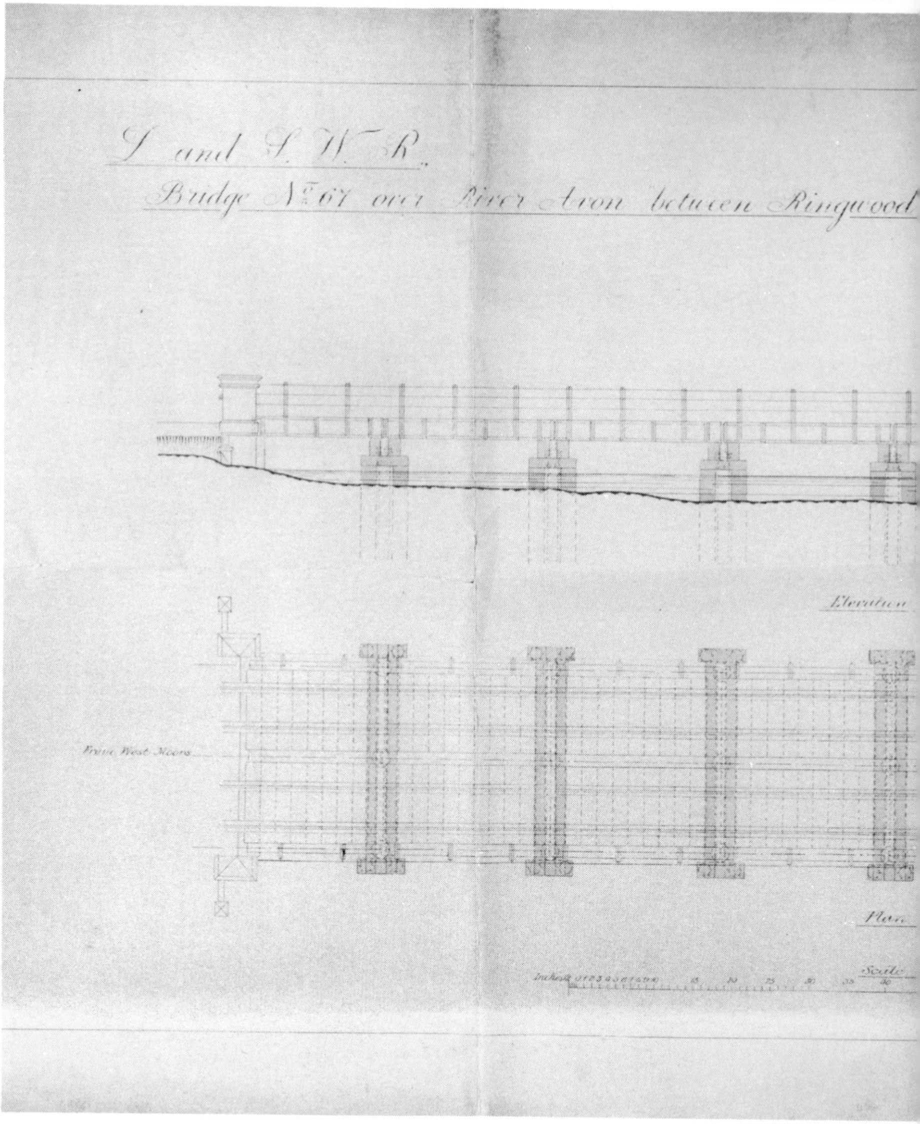

L and S.W.R.

Bridge N.º 67 over River Avon between Ringwood

Elevation

From West Moors

Plan

Scale

Existing piles and crossheads are shown dotted and coloured black

Proposed new piles and crossheads are coloured red

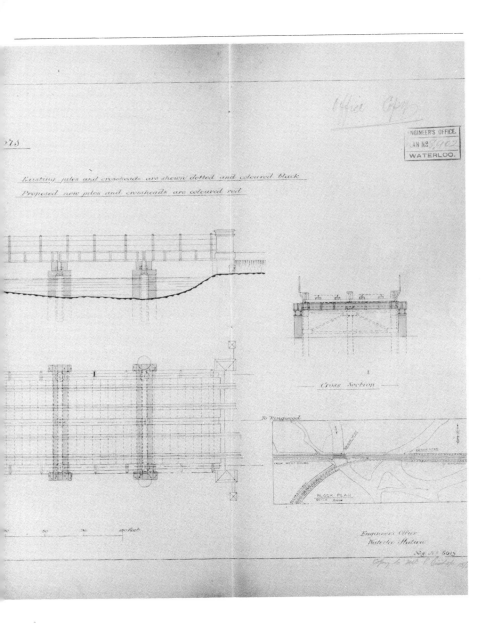

Cross Section

Block Plan

Engineer's Office
Waterloo Station

Neg No 5015

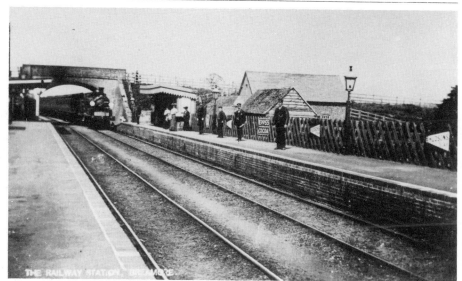

ON THE ONCE IMPORTANT THROUGH LINE from Salisbury to West Moors this is Breamore station. Notice the fashion of placing the station buildings at one end of the platform for ease of access from the bridge which was also evident at Fleet earlier in this book. (Lens of Sutton.)

CONCLUDING THIS BRIEF LOOK at the mainland railways of Hampshire is this fine study of Fordingbridge, also on the line south from Salisbury. Throughout the course of its path the earthworks for the railway were built for a double line of rails although these were only laid at the various crossing stations; intended for an expansion which was never to come. The site at Fordingbridge has now vanished under an industrial estate. Further views of the northern section of this line are to be found in the companion volume *Wiltshire Railways in Old Photographs*.

Hampshire Railways in Old Photographs
Kevin Robertson

Over the last 50 years the railways of Hampshire have undergone considerable change. The steam engine is now a thing of the past on ordinary passenger lines and the lines themselves have undergone major reorganization and rationalization. This collection of photographs provides an interesting pictorial history of the railway network of Hampshire.

Kevin Robertson is the author of several railway books and has already written about the branch lines of this county. The additional pictorial material used in this volume will make this book enjoyable for those who knew the Hampshire railways in their heyday, for railway enthusiasts and the residents of Hampshire alike.

ISBN 0-86299-668-6

9 780862 996680

Sutton Publishing Limited
Phoenix Mill · Stroud · Gloucestershire